MEL BAY PRESENTS

FOR RECORDER

AN EARLY AMERICAN CHRISTMAS

THE CHARM OF A COLONIAL YULETIDE

A recording of the music in this book is now available. The publisher strongly recommends the use of this recording along with the text to insure accuracy of interpretation and ease in learning.

In conjunction with Green Hill

CONTENTS

INTRODUCTION

The companion recording to this book by the same title contains pieces I have arranged for a variety of instrumentation (string quartet, guitars, recorders, and penny whistle). From these original arrangements, I have transcribed the selections in this book specifically for the recorder player.

Due to the variety of the original instrumentation, some of the pieces have been placed in a key different from the recording, and the form of a few has been adapted to better suit the solo performance.

Enjoy.

- John Mock

JOY TO THE WORLD

Arr. by John Mock

THE CHERRY TREE CAROL

Arr. by John Mock

Soprano Record

WHILE SHEPHERDS WATCHED
THEIR FLOCKS

Arr. by John Mock

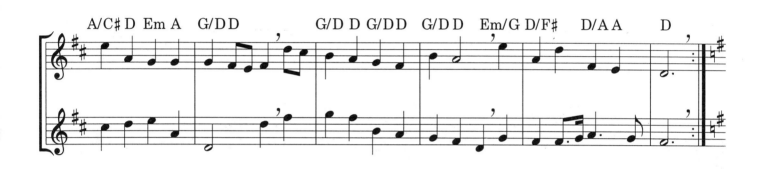

THE HOLLY AND THE IVY

Arr. by John Mock

THE PARTING GLASS

Arr. by John Mock

Soprano Recorder

HARK! THE HERALD ANGELS SING

Arr. by John Mock

The Angels

13

BOSTON

Arr. by John Mock

Alto Recorder

WHAT CHILD IS THIS

Arr. by John Mock

Alto Recorder

SWEET SLUMBERS

Recorder Duet

Arr. by John Mock

THE HOLLY HILL

Arr. by John Mock

Soprano Recorder

THE COVENTRY CAROL
PACKINGTON'S POUND

Arr. by John Mock

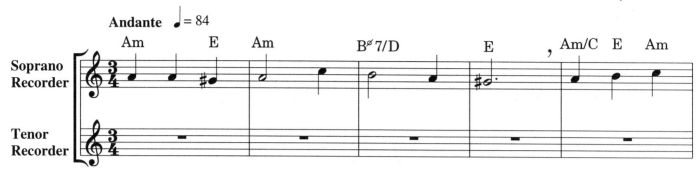

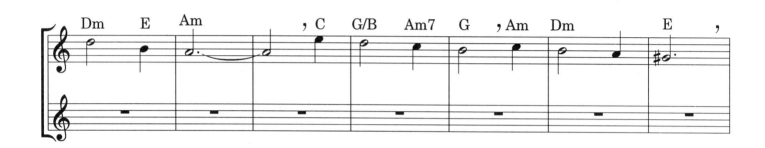

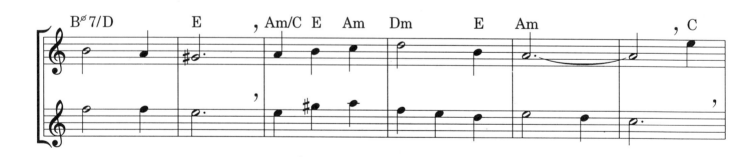

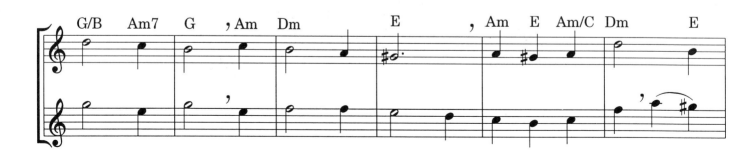

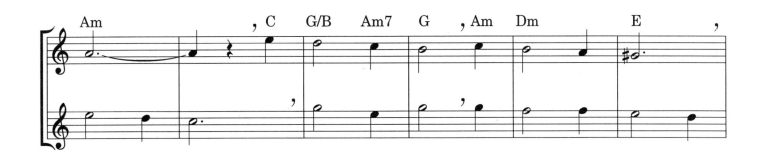

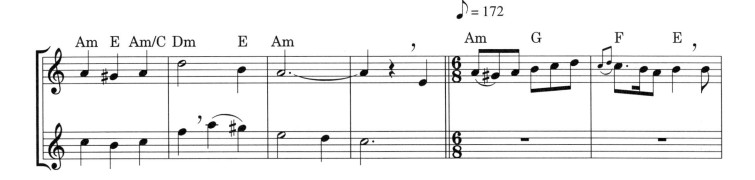

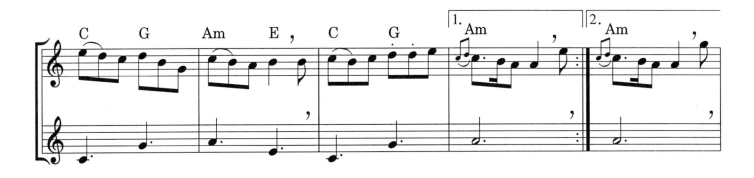

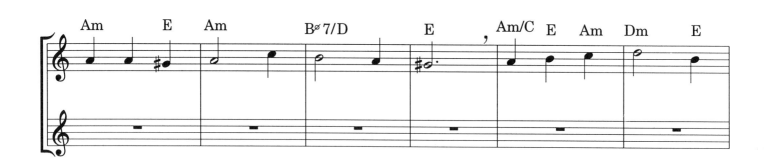
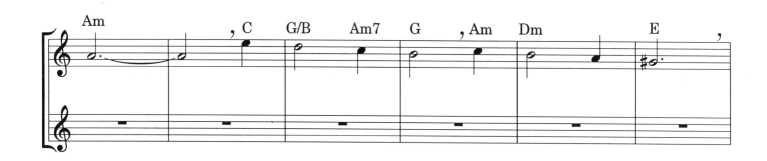
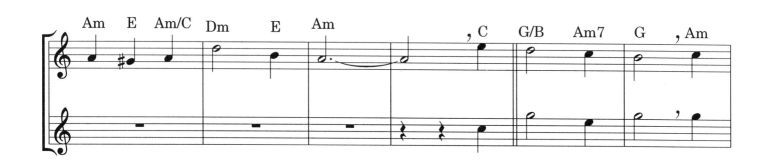
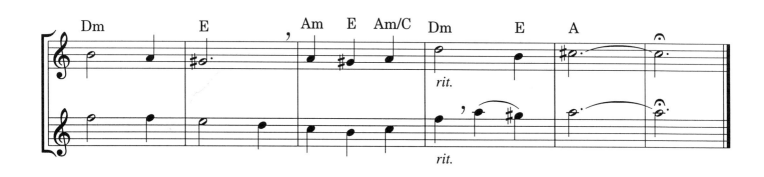

20

GOD REST YE MERRY GENTLEMEN

Arr. by John Mock

Soprano Recorder

Fine

D.S. al Fine

BOSTON
(Reprise)

Arr. by John Mock

Soprano Recorder

D.S. al Fine

MERRY

CHRISTMAS